CLASSIFIED

WORLD WAR II
SPIES

BY SEAN STEWART PRICE

Consultant:
Jan Goldman, EdD
Founding Board Member
International Intelligence Ethics Association
Washington, D.C.

CAPSTONE PRESS
a capstone imprint

Velocity Books are published by Capstone Press,
1710 Roe Crest Drive, North Mankato, Minnesota 56003
www.capstonepub.com

Library of Congress Cataloging-in-Publication Data
Price, Sean.
World War II spies / by Sean Stewart Price.
pages cm. — (Classified)
Summary: "Describes the activities of famous spies of World War II"— Provided by
publisher.
ISBN 978-1-4765-0122-2 (library binding)
ISBN 978-1-4765-3588-3 (ebook PDF)
1. World War, 1939-1945—Secret service—Juvenile literature. 2. Espionage—History—20th
century—Juvenile literature. 3. Spies—History—20th century—Juvenile literature. I. Title. II.
Title: World War Two spies. III. Title: World War 2 spies.
D810.S7P76 2014
940.54′850922—dc23   2012046431

Editorial Credits
Mandy Robbins, editor; Veronica Scott, designer; Jennifer Walker, production specialist

Photo Credits
Alamy: Daily Mail/Rex, 11, INTERFOTO, 7, 19, 24, World History Archive, 29; Corbis, 4, 17,
39, Bettmann, 32-33, 35, Hulton-Deutsch Collection, 31, 36; National Archives and Records
Administration, 13; Newscom/akg-images, 9 (inset), 22-23; Shutterstock: Dja65, 27 (camera),
Dmitriy Lesnyak, 36-37, Everett Collection, cover, Gary Blakeley, 43, 44, 45 (flags), Jemny,
20-21, 40-41, Kartinkin77, 26 (phone), Marques, 16-17, Olemac, 10 (bottom), 28 (patches),
panbazil, 10 (top), Pjasha, 20, 25, 30 (map), ssuaphotos, 26-27, Steshkin Yevgeniy, 4 (inset),
steve estvanik, 12,13, 14, 15 (ships), Sundan, 14-15, Torsten Lorenz, 42 (both), Tushnov
Alexey, 8-9, twobluedogs, 28, udra11, 4-5 (map), ULKASTUDIO, 18, 38-39; Wikimedia, 12,
15, 16 (portrait), 19 (press pass), Amephoto, 41 (portrait), Moyzischewitz, 21 (inset)

Artistic Effects
Shutterstock

Printed in the United States of America in North Mankato, Minnesota.
032013   007223CGF13

TABLE OF CONTENTS

A WORLD AT WAR

During the 1930s, a recipe for war was brewing. In Germany, Adolf Hitler's Nazi Party rose to power. The Nazis promised to help the country bounce back from its defeat in World War I (1914–1918). They also promised to restore national pride and give people jobs and food. But once the Nazis took over Germany's government in 1933, they set out to conquer Europe.

German soldiers drive through Poland in 1939.

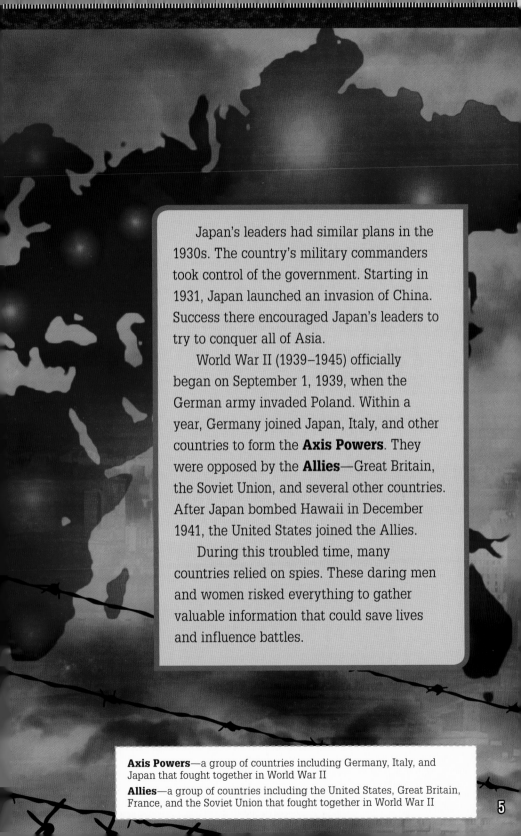

Japan's leaders had similar plans in the 1930s. The country's military commanders took control of the government. Starting in 1931, Japan launched an invasion of China. Success there encouraged Japan's leaders to try to conquer all of Asia.

World War II (1939–1945) officially began on September 1, 1939, when the German army invaded Poland. Within a year, Germany joined Japan, Italy, and other countries to form the **Axis Powers**. They were opposed by the **Allies**—Great Britain, the Soviet Union, and several other countries. After Japan bombed Hawaii in December 1941, the United States joined the Allies.

During this troubled time, many countries relied on spies. These daring men and women risked everything to gather valuable information that could save lives and influence battles.

Axis Powers—a group of countries including Germany, Italy, and Japan that fought together in World War II

Allies—a group of countries including the United States, Great Britain, France, and the Soviet Union that fought together in World War II

HIDING IN PLAIN SIGHT

On November 23, 1940, a French train stopped as it crossed the border between France and Spain. In peacetime, this would have been a simple matter. But just five months earlier, Hitler's armies had taken control of France. German border guards stepped onto the train looking for anyone suspicious. They especially wanted to find spies leaving the country who could pass information to enemies.

Josephine Baker was on the train. She was a world–famous African-American singer and dancer. Baker wore a huge fur coat and looked every bit the glamorous star she was. Next to her stood a plain-looking man carrying her suitcase. The guards waved Baker and her friend through and into Spain. Once in Spain, the pair caught a plane to Lisbon, Portugal.

AN AMERICAN IN PARIS

Baker fled the United States as a young woman because of the **racism** there. In the 1920s, she traveled to Paris, the capital of France, where blacks were more accepted. Her singing and dancing made her a sensation. Baker put on flashy shows. She dressed dramatically and appeared on stage with a cheetah. Baker was the first African-American woman to become a worldwide celebrity.

Baker became a French citizen and lived in France when the Germans invaded. When French Army Captain Jacques Abtey asked her to be a spy, Baker said "They [the people of Paris] have given me their hearts, and I have given them mine. I am ready, Captain, to give them my life."

JOSEPHINE BAKER

racism—prejudice or discrimination against people of a different race

SECRET MESSAGES

The man accompanying Baker on the train was actually Captain Abtey. Once in Lisbon, Baker and Abtey made contact with British officials. They had some secrets to share. Pinned in Baker's dress were photos showing the strength of the German army in France. The sheet music in her suitcase also contained important secrets written in invisible ink. Facts and figures about the German forces were written on each page.

Baker and Abtey could have been stopped and searched by the police or by the Gestapo, Hitler's secret police. If that had happened, they would have been arrested and possibly killed.

Abtey had worried about using Baker as a spy at first. Any doubts he had vanished quickly. "You see what a good **cover** I am?" Baker kidded Abtey after their mission was over.

Josephine Baker, 1930

FACT:

The Gestapo's job was to crush all opposition to Nazi rule. Gestapo agents could arrest people without warning. Often those people were killed or ended up in **concentration camps**.

cover—a fake name or story that a spy uses to conceal his or her identity and stay safe

concentration camp—a prison camp where thousands of inmates are held under extremely harsh conditions

'NOBODY WILL THINK I'M A SPY'

Baker had become a spy even before the Germans invaded France. She had worked for France's military intelligence. Baker knew many political leaders. They included **diplomats** for Italy and Japan.

Baker frequently went to parties held for Italian and Japanese diplomats. She reported back what she had heard. Sometimes she heard so much that she would write things on her arms and hands to remember them. Abtey later warned her that this could be dangerous. "Oh, nobody will think I'm a spy," she said.

After the Germans invaded, Baker continued to work as a messenger for the French **resistance**. She frequently brought information to Allies in other parts of Europe and North Africa.

diplomat—a person who officially represents one country in another country
resistance—people working secretly against occupying forces

THE FORTUNE OF FAME

Adolf Hitler and the Nazis believed Germans were the "master race." They looked down on other people, especially Jewish people and blacks. Whenever Germans invaded a country, they rounded up people who belonged to these groups. The Nazis sent them to concentration camps. Millions died there.

Josephine Baker was black and married to a Jewish man. She was in special danger, but her fame kept her from being arrested. She used that fame to gain travel papers for many Jewish friends and acquaintances. Her efforts helped them escape the Nazis.

JAPAN'S SECRET WEAPON

At 7:55 a.m. on December 7, 1941, Takeo Yoshikawa was eating breakfast. It was a beautiful, sunny day on the Hawaiian Island of Oahu. Suddenly, the sounds of explosions and gunfire rocked the peaceful morning.

Most people on Oahu were shocked. They raced outside to find out what was going on. But Yoshikawa already had a pretty good idea. He knew that Japanese planes from nearby aircraft carriers were attacking the island's naval base, Pearl Harbor. The U.S. Pacific fleet was anchored there. Japan's leaders hoped to wipe out U.S. naval power in the Pacific with one swift, surprise attack.

THE PAYOFF

For Yoshikawa, the attack was the payoff for eight months of work. He was a Japanese spy, and his expert snooping had helped make the attack possible. Japan's military sent Yoshikawa to watch Pearl Harbor daily. He reported how many ships were there and when they came and left. He scouted out nearby military airfields to see how many planes were there. And he watched Americans' activities and attitudes to see if they were prepared for an attack. They weren't.

The attack on Pearl Harbor killed 2,403 Americans, including 68 civilians.

SAILOR TO SPY

The Japanese had other spies at Pearl Harbor, but Yoshikawa was by far their best. He didn't start off his career as a spy, though. As a young man, Yoshikawa served in the Japanese Navy. He was a successful officer. But a stomach ailment forced him to quit the military. Then he got a second chance. The Japanese Navy's spy branch asked him to join.

Yoshikawa quickly became an expert on U.S. ships. He could recognize any warship just by looking at its profile. In the spring of 1941, Yoshikawa was sent to Hawaii. He arrived in Oahu under the cover name Tadashi Morimura. His cover was that he worked at the Japanese government's **consulate** in Hawaii. "Morimura" was officially a diplomat. But he spent little time at his desk job. By day, he traveled around Oahu's military sites. By night, he sent back reports on them to Tokyo.

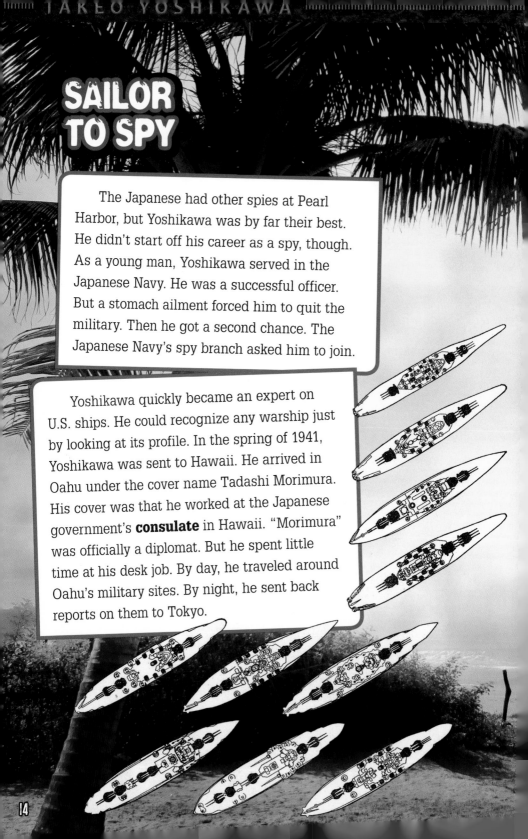

BLENDING IN

Hawaii had a large population of Japanese-Americans. Also, Asian tourists flocked to Hawaii for its natural beauty. So Yoshikawa blended right in. But he also found ways to sneak onto military bases in disguise. One time he pretended to be a dishwasher. That allowed him to overhear conversations at an officer's club.

Takeo Yoshikawa

But Yoshikawa really didn't need to do anything illegal. Almost all the planes and ships he kept track of were in plain sight.

"The Americans were very foolish," Yoshikawa would recall later. "As a diplomat I could move about the islands freely. I often rented small planes at John Rodgers Airport in Honolulu and flew around observing U.S. [military sites]. I never took notes or drew maps. I kept everything in my head."

consulate—official building or buildings for foreign diplomats

VITAL INFORMATION

Yoshikawa's information shaped the Pearl Harbor attack. He told those planning the raid the best routes for planes to fly in undetected. He showed them how the U.S. ships and planes would be lined up. He even told them that Sunday was the harbor's most crowded day. So that determined the day of the event.

Yoshikawa's work led to the most one-sided attack in U.S. military history. The 90-minute ambush killed almost 2,400 U.S. servicemen and wounded another 1,200. It also sank or damaged 21 ships. They included eight battleships. More than 300 aircraft were damaged or destroyed. In return the Japanese lost only 64 lives. Most were airmen who were shot down.

An overhead view of Pearl Harbor before the Japanese attacked

Almost as soon as the attack was over, angry Americans surrounded the Japanese consulate on Hawaii. Police held them back. Meanwhile, Yoshikawa and other officials inside the consulate burned code books and important papers. They were soon arrested and held for several days. Then they were exchanged for U.S. diplomats that had been held by the Japanese. U.S. officials didn't realize until after the war that they had held the spy who had made the Pearl Harbor attack possible.

SOVIET MASTER SPY

Early on May 13, 1938, Richard Sorge lost control of his motorcycle. He smashed the motorcycle into a wall near his home in Tokyo, Japan. Sorge survived, but he was in agonizing pain. People heard the crash and rushed to his aid. Despite his pain, Sorge waved them off. He kept saying, "Tell Clausen to come at once."

What his rescuers did not know was that Sorge was a spy for the Soviet Union. Max Clausen was a fellow spy. Sorge had important intelligence documents in his pocket. He needed to give them to Clausen for safekeeping. Sorge feared that doctors would find them and report them to the police. If that happened, he would be arrested.

By the time Clausen reached his friend, Sorge's condition had gotten worse.

"He was unable to speak," Clausen remembered, "but even then he had his wits about him. Only after he had handed me the important confidential papers ... only when these were safely in my hands, did he lose consciousness."

This incident shows many of the things that made Sorge a great spy. He was tough, determined, and willing to take chances.

RICHARD SORGE

氏名...... Richard Sorge

Frankfurter

Zeitung

FACT:

Sorge's cover was that he was a German journalist working for the newspaper *Frankfurter Zeitung*. This cover allowed him to snoop and pry without arousing suspicion.

A RING OF SPIES

Sorge is widely seen as one of the greatest spies in history. His biggest accomplishment was setting up a **spy ring** in Tokyo. At that time, the Japanese did not trust outsiders. Most foreigners were not welcome. Few were allowed to live there.

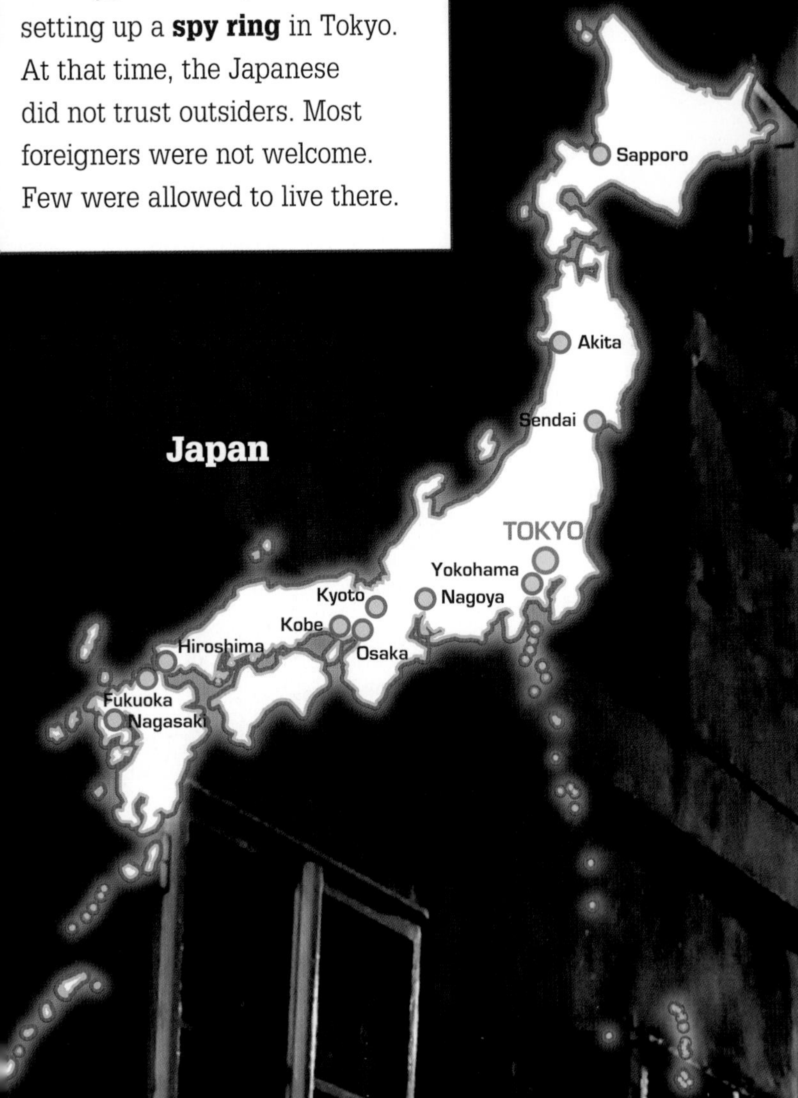

Japan

Sapporo

Akita

Sendai

TOKYO

Yokohama

Kyoto

Nagoya

Kobe

Hiroshima

Osaka

Fukuoka

Nagasaki

Sorge got away with it because he was German. Germany and Japan were friendly in the 1930s. Japanese officials and other Germans living in Tokyo thought Sorge supported Adolf Hitler. This mistaken belief opened doors to Sorge. High-level officials trusted him and other spies in his ring.

From 1933 to 1941, Sorge's spy ring sent many valuable secrets to the Soviet Union. Members of Sorge's spy ring learned important secrets about German and Japanese military strength and troop movements.

Eugen Ott

FACT:

One of Sorge's best sources was Germany's ambassador to Japan, Eugen Ott. The two men were close, and Sorge was an expert on Japanese affairs. Ott sometimes even handed Sorge top-secret documents and asked for his opinion.

spy ring—a group of people who secretly collect information about enemies
ambassador—the top representative, or diplomat, of one country living in another country

THE BIGGEST SCOOP

Sorge's greatest moment came in 1941. At that time, Germany and the Soviet Union were at peace. But Sorge found out that Germany planned to invade the Soviet Union. He even pinned down the date—June 22.

But Soviet **dictator** Joseph Stalin ignored Sorge's warning. He did not want to believe that Germany was willing to break the peace. As a result, the Soviet army was caught by surprise when the Germans did invade on June 22.

Sorge was angry about being ignored. But he helped Stalin recover from this terrible blunder. In the fall of 1941, German armies approached Moscow from the west. It looked as though the Soviet government would fall. Stalin needed more troops to fight Hitler. But he also feared that Japan might invade the Soviet Union from the east.

Sorge found out from his contacts that Japan was not planning to attack the Soviet Union. This time Stalin believed Sorge. Stalin took armies from the east and sent them west to face the Germans. This last-minute switch probably saved Moscow.

UNDER ARREST

But Sorge could not enjoy this triumph. Japan's police had received a tip about Sorge's ring. Many of Sorge's spies were captured and forced to tell authorities about Sorge's spying. In October 1941, the Japanese arrested Sorge early one morning, taking him away in pajamas. His spy ring was out of action.

German troops march into the Soviet Union on June 22, 1941.

dictator—someone who has complete control of a country, often ruling it unjustly

GERMANY'S BEST AGENT

Fear gripped Ludwig Moyzisch as he looked in his rearview mirror. A car was chasing him through the streets of Ankara, the capital of Turkey. Moyzisch was a diplomat for Germany. In his backseat was the Nazi's best spy, Elyesa Bazna.

FACT:

Bazna's German code name was "Cicero," the same name as a famous public speaker from ancient Rome.

Turkey

Samsun

Istanbul
Kocaeli
Trabzon

Bursa
Erzurum

Balikesir
Eskisehir
○ANKARA
Sivas

Manisa
Izmir
Kayseri
Van

Konya
Diyarbakir

Antalya
Kahramanmaras
Adana
Gaziantep
Mersin
Sanliurfa

Antakya

Moyzisch was afraid that the person in the car would spot him with Bazna. If that happened, Bazna's cover would be blown. Bazna worked as a servant in the British embassy in Turkey. British embassy servants simply didn't drive around with German diplomats. If seen together, everyone would know that Bazna was a German spy.

Moyzisch sped up. He turned corners quickly. He zoomed dangerously through the streets of Ankara. In the backseat, a sweating, nervous Bazna chewed his nails.

Finally, Moyzisch saw a possible escape. He made a quick turn. As he did, he slowed down just enough for Bazna to jump out. Bazna rolled out of the car on the ground. "[I] found myself lying flat on my face in the shadow of a garden fence," Bazna later wrote. He looked up to see if he could identify the pursuer as he drove by. But all he saw was "a shadow crouching over the steering wheel."

SELLING SECRETS

Despite the scare, Bazna's identity was safe. He was able to continue working as a servant for the British ambassador to Turkey. For the past several months, Bazna had been photographing the ambassador's secret documents. They revealed key information about British troop movements and war goals. Germans like Moyzisch were anxious to find out those secrets. Bazna himself did not actually care about the Nazi cause. He just wanted to become rich, so he sold his photographs to the Germans. Bazna and Moyzisch usually met in Moyzisch's car. They were in the middle of a sale when interrupted by their pursuer.

Bazna was a daring spy. But the ambassador made his task easy for him. The ambassador took few security measures. He often brought top-secret government papers home to read. Sometimes he left them on his desk. The ambassador also used sleeping pills. That meant Bazna could sneak around the sleeping man without waking him up.

TOP SECRET

TOO GOOD TO BE TRUE?

Bazna even got keys to the ambassador's safe. This access allowed him to photograph even more information and sell it to Moyzisch. Many German officials valued Bazna's information. Hitler himself promised to buy Bazna a new home after the war.

But there were also German leaders who mistrusted this agent, known only to them as Cicero. They thought the information he obtained was too good to be true. They feared that the British were trying to set them up by using a phony spy. German leaders also argued over how to use Cicero's information. As a result, it seldom had a big impact on German decisions.

END OF THE ROAD

Bazna's career as a spy came to an end in early 1944. Allied spies tipped off the Americans that the British embassy in Ankara had a spy. Security at the embassy tightened. Bazna found it harder to gain information. He soon stopped spying altogether.

During the time Bazna was a spy, Turkey was **neutral** in World War II. Then in August 1944, Turkey broke off diplomatic relations with Germany and declared war. As a German, Moyzisch was considered an enemy of Turkey. He was arrested and spent the rest of the war in prison camp.

Adolf Hitler and other German leaders receive salutes as they march through a German street.

neutral—not taking sides in a conflict

MADAM TSUBAKI

In 1942 Club Tsubaki in Manila was one of the most popular nightspots in the Philippines. The owner, Madam Tsubaki, had a talent for charming Japanese army officers. These high-ranking soldiers were part of a huge Japanese force taking over the Pacific. They had just driven the U.S. Army and Navy out of the Philippines.

Philippines

BATAN IS.

Luzon Strait

BABUYAN IS.

Laoag

LUZON

PHILIPPINE SEA

Dagupan

Quezon City

MANILA

MINDORO

Legazpi

SAMAR

BUSUANGA I.

Tacloban

SOUTH CHINA SEA

PANAY

LEYTE

Cebu

NEGROS

PALAWAN

Sulu Sea

CEBU

BOHOL

MINDANAO

Zamboanga

Davao

JOLO I.

General Santos

BASILAN I.

SULU ARCHIPELAGO

Manila was destroyed by fighting at the end of the war.

Madam Tsubaki sang and danced onstage for her customers. She liked to talk with them about their work. Madam Tsubaki was a beautiful and friendly woman. She seemed to really care about the soldiers. She even offered to introduce one lonely captain to local people so that he could make friends.

"No can do," the captain replied. "I'm going to the Lingayen Gulf."

"The Lingayen Gulf," Madam Tsubaki echoed. "Why should the army send you way up there, where it's quiet and peaceful?"

"You women don't understand war," said the captain, smiling. "We Japanese landed at that place and found it easy to take [from the Americans]. Americans may have the same idea. We're keeping many soldiers there. Now you understand?"

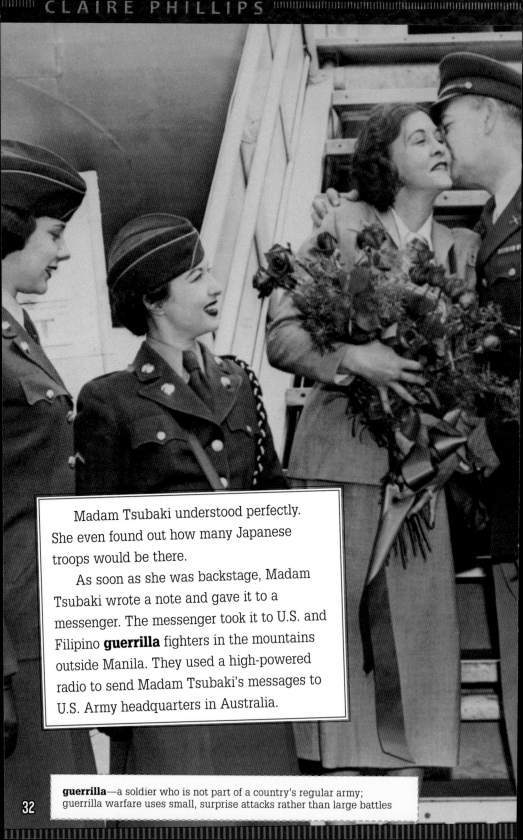

Madam Tsubaki understood perfectly. She even found out how many Japanese troops would be there.

As soon as she was backstage, Madam Tsubaki wrote a note and gave it to a messenger. The messenger took it to U.S. and Filipino **guerrilla** fighters in the mountains outside Manila. They used a high-powered radio to send Madam Tsubaki's messages to U.S. Army headquarters in Australia.

guerrilla—a soldier who is not part of a country's regular army; guerrilla warfare uses small, surprise attacks rather than large battles

Madam Tsubaki's real name was Claire Phillips. She was an American and the wife of a U.S. soldier in the Philippines. Her husband had died shortly after the Japanese invasion of the Philippines. Phillips had been an actress and a singer before the war. So she opened up her nightclub and took the name Madam Tsubaki. Phillips hadn't been able to help her own husband. So she vowed to help other soldiers who were still fighting the Japanese.

Claire Phillips was given a hero's welcome when she returned to the United States after the war.

PRISON LIFE

Phillips was also committed to helping U.S. prisoners of war being held by the Japanese on the Philippines. Life in Japanese prison camps was brutal. Inmates were forced to work hard in the blazing sun while given little food or clothing. Phillips used money she earned from her club to buy supplies for prisoners at the nearby Japanese prison camp. At great personal risk, she made sure that food, medicine, and letters made it into the camp. Those items often meant the difference between life and death for prisoners.

In May 1944, the Japanese police caught up with Phillips. They tracked her down from a note she'd left a prisoner. After being tortured and questioned, Phillips was imprisoned in Manila's harsh Bilibid prison. She was close to starvation when American forces freed her in February 1945.

American prisoners of war near Manila sip water in the blazing sun.

THE THANKS OF STARVING MEN

Phillips' efforts raised prisoners' spirits. One letter to her from a prisoner read:

Hello High-Pockets: When I got your letter, I came to life again. Gee, it's good to know someone like you. You've done more for the boys' morale in here than you'll ever know.

TAKING ON THE NAZIS

Gunnar Sonsteby rang the doorbell of a friend's apartment. As he did so, he got the feeling that something was wrong. Maybe the glow from the window was too bright. Maybe it was just the sense for danger that he had developed. Sonsteby had already spent years working for the resistance in Norway. These people fought secretly against the German Nazis, who had invaded in April 1940.

A newspaper seller displays the news that Germany has invaded Norway.

The door opened and Sonsteby's fears were confirmed. He was staring down the barrel of a handgun.

Sonsteby acted immediately. He yelled and knocked the pistol aside. Then he ran down the entryway stairs to the street. Two shots rang out. Sonsteby was just a few feet away. But it was dark, and he was running. The shots missed him.

A MISSING NOTEBOOK

Sonsteby had a friend waiting in a nearby car. He jumped in, and they sped off. But the excitement of their narrow escape was short-lived. In the dash away from the door, Sonsteby had dropped a notebook. He couldn't remember if there was anything important in it. But he couldn't risk having it fall into German hands.

GOING BACK

Sonsteby changed clothes and went back to the apartment building. This time he held his own pistol tightly in his pocket. Sonsteby was ready to shoot at any sign of trouble. As he walked along the front of the building, he spotted the notebook lying at the edge of a snow bank. Sonsteby picked it up quickly and kept walking.

Daring acts such as these made Sonsteby one of the leaders of Norway's resistance during World War II. He dodged the Germans for five years. They didn't even know his true identity until near the end of the war. Sonsteby traveled through street **checkpoints** with fake identity papers. He was constantly on the move and almost never slept in the same place two nights in a row. Sonsteby took bicycles and cabs all around Oslo, Norway's capital, during the day. He arranged meetings with other resistance members in stores and restaurants.

Sonsteby and his friends were dedicated to helping Norwegian citizens. The resistance smuggled people out of the country to neighboring Sweden. That country was neutral in the war. Resistance members also stole food ration booklets to keep people from starving. Sonsteby's men even helped steal the printing plates used to make Norwegian money. The plates were copied for the British and quickly replaced. This allowed the British to print Norwegian money to help pay for the resistance.

The Germans hung Nazi symbols throughout Oslo.

FACT:

Sonsteby operated under at least 30 different names to hide his identity.

checkpoint—a place where authorities stop people to ask for identification and to look for suspicious people

SEEKING SONSTEBY

Eventually, the Germans discovered Sonsteby's identity and launched a huge manhunt. He escaped to Great Britain, but only to train for more action. Sonsteby learned how to use explosives and other weapons. His training helped him destroy targets in Norway that were important to the Germans.

Sonsteby parachuted into Norway in November 1943 and began leading a group of resistance fighters. They destroyed German records, weapons factories, planes, and ships. In June 1944, the Allies invaded France to drive out the Nazis. Sonsteby's unit destroyed railways that kept German soldiers in Norway from reaching the front lines.

In April 1945, the war was winding down. Germany was clearly losing. Germans and their Norwegian allies began destroying their records of killings and arrests. They didn't want to be punished for their deeds after the war. Sonsteby's unit captured many of the official German papers before they were destroyed. This way, Nazi leaders could be identified and punished.

The war in Europe ended when Germany surrendered on May 7, 1945. Sonsteby could not believe it. "The time was over when I had to go about with an innocent poker face calling myself Krogh or Fjeld or Berg, knowing that the Gestapo were hunting me. I could be myself and let everyone know that I was I—Gunnar Sonsteby."

Gunnar Sonsteby in 2008

THE NAZIS STRIKE BACK

The Germans knew that resistance fighters operated with support from ordinary Norwegians. They tried to stop that by punishing people randomly. In February 1945, the resistance killed a high-level Nazi on an Oslo street. The Germans responded by rounding up nearly 30 innocent Norwegians and executing them.

END OF THE WAR

Although the fighting in Europe ended in May 1945, the war in the Pacific dragged on for several more months. World War II finally ended on August 14, 1945. Nobody is sure how many soldiers and civilians died in the war. Many estimates put the total at 50 million people, but the real number may be much higher.

Some spies who survived the war continued to work as secret agents. But most World War II spies were ordinary people before the war. They gave up the undercover life once peace returned. You may be wondering the fates of the spies featured in this book.

JOSEPHINE BAKER (1906–1975)

Josephine Baker received the Croix de Guerre (Cross of War) for her work in the French resistance. It is one of France's highest military honors. She also won the Medal of Resistance. As Baker grew older, she became a strong supporter of the civil rights movement in the United States during the 1950s and 1960s.

TAKEO YOSHIKAWA (1914–1993)

After Japan lost the war, Yoshikawa went into hiding. American troops occupied Japan for several years. He feared they would hurt him. Even after Yoshikawa revealed himself, other Japanese wanted nothing to do with him. Many blamed him for the Pearl Harbor attack. They saw the attack as the cause of the war that ended in Japan's defeat. Even Japan's government refused to acknowledge his work, declining to give him military benefits. Yoshikawa lived the rest of his life bitter toward the Japanese government.

RICHARD SORGE (1895–1944)

Sorge was imprisoned in Japan after his arrest. The Japanese expected the Soviets to trade Sorge for a Japanese spy caught in the Soviet Union. This kind of trade is normal among countries. But Soviet dictator Joseph Stalin refused to trade. Historians believe he did not want Sorge around after the war. Sorge would be able to prove that Stalin had ignored his warning about the German invasion. The Japanese hanged Sorge in 1944.

ELYESA BAZNA (1904–1970)

Bazna was the highest paid spy in history up to that time. He received up to $1.2 million for his work. Today that would be equal to about $16 million. But there was a catch. Bazna insisted on being paid in British money, called pounds. The British pounds the Germans used were mostly **counterfeit**. When Bazna tried to spend this money after the war, banks refused to accept it. Bazna ended up quite poor.

counterfeit—something fake that looks like the real thing

CLAIRE
PHILLIPS (1908–1960)

Phillips returned to the United States after being rescued from prison. She was given a Presidential Medal of Freedom, the highest award an American civilian can get. A movie and a book were made about her adventures. Even with this publicity, most people quickly forgot about her. But the prisoners she helped never did.

GUNNAR
SONSTEBY (1918–2012)

Sonsteby became one of Norway's most famous war heroes. He won Norway's War Cross with Three Swords, the British Distinguished Service Order, and the U.S. Medal of Freedom. In May 2007 Norway's King Harald unveiled a statue of Sonsteby in Oslo. The statue shows a young Sonsteby standing next to the bicycle he used to ride around Oslo during the war.

GLOSSARY

Allies (AL-eyz)—a group of countries including the United States, Great Britain, France, Russia, and Italy that fought together in World War II

ambassador (am-BA-suh-duhr)—the top representative, or diplomat, of one country living in another country

Axis Powers (AK-siss POU-urz)—a group of countries including Germany, Italy, and Japan that fought together in World War II

checkpoint (CHEK-point)—a place where authorities stop people to ask for identification and to look for suspicious people

concentration camp (kahn-suhn-TRAY-shuhn KAMP)—a prison camp where thousands of inmates are held under harsh conditions

consulate (KON-suh-luht)—official building or buildings for foreign diplomats

counterfeit (KOUN-tuhr-fit)—something fake that looks like the real thing, such as counterfeit money

cover (KUH-ver)—a fake name or story that a spy uses to conceal his or her identity and stay safe

dictator (DIK-tay-tuhr)—someone who has complete control of a country, often ruling it unjustly

diplomat (DIP-luh-mat)—a person who officially represents one country in another country

guerrilla (guh-RIL-ah)—a soldier who is not part of a country's regular army; guerrilla warfare involves small, surprise attacks rather than large battles

neutral (NOO-truhl)—not taking sides in a conflict

racism (RAY-siz-uhm)—prejudice or discrimination against people of a different race

resistance (ri-ZISS-tuhnss)—people working secretly against occupying forces

spy ring (SPYE RING)—a group of people who secretly collect information about enemies

READ MORE

Burgan, Michael. *World War II Spies: an Interactive History Adventure.* You Choose. North Mankato, Minn.: Capstone Press, 2013.

Malam, John. *You Wouldn't Want to Be a Secret Agent During World War II!: A Perilous Mission Behind Enemy Lines.* London, United Kingdom: Franklin Watts, 2010.

O'Shei, Tim. *World War II Spies.* Spies. Mankato, Minn.: Capstone Press, 2008.

INTERNET SITES

FactHound offers a safe, fun way to find Internet sites related to this book. All of the sites on FactHound have been researched by our staff.

Here's all you do:

Visit *www.facthound.com*

Type in this code: 9781476501222

INDEX